MODERN
ACROSTICS

Ken
Waldman

MODERN
ACROSTICS

Ken
Waldman

Ridgeway Press
Roseville, Michigan

Ridgeway Press
P.O. Box 120, Roseville MI 48066

Acknowledgments:
This was the culmination of many years of writing and travel. Thanks to the many who invited me to their communities. Without those invitations, I wouldn't/couldn't have written so many of the poems here.

While I've privately circulated some of these acrostic poems over the years, a few found their way in journals. Those are listed below. I thank those editors.

Big thanks here to M.L. Liebler of Ridgeway Press whose support as publisher has been crucial.

Then there are those who had poems dedicated to them. And behind the scenes have been other friends and colleagues whose contributions I especially want to mention by name: Lucy Long, Mark Striffler, Becky Levy, Stephen Sunderlin, Richard Wolfe. Apologies to the many friends and colleagues whose names I've omitted. I've had a lot of help from a lot of directions.

eMerge: "Frank Soos" "Robin Metz" "Jeff Day, Pilot" "McKean
    County" "Whiskey" "Salina, Kansas" "Winter Solstice"
Molecule: "Route 50"
Rattle: "F. Wayne Scott"
Whistlepig: "Mountain Home" "Mountain Home, Idaho"
Dear Butte Anthology: "Montana" "Dear Butte[2]"

Table of Contents

for Elizabeth English, patron of the arts

This collection is the direct result of a crowdfunding campaign. Every one of these backers helped make this print edition a reality: Paul Fericano, Rachael Fulbright & Charlie Carew, Elizabeth English, Hal & Lisa Tovin, Mark Tamsula, Barbara Rosner, Suzanne Todd, Stephanie Dickie, David Epley, Jennifer Spector, Sidney Myer, Alexis Knudsen, Jim Kruger, Sallie Mack & Jonathan Freese, Llysa Holland, Emily Pinkerton, Jamie Hascall, Jordan Wankoff, Jerry Hagins, Beth Chrisman, Eric Graves, Rich Russell, Cheryl Chrisman, Caitlin Warbelow, David McCormick, Maureen Kelly, Ellen Ferguson, Claire Holland LeClair, John Carnahan, Jay Best, Anne-Marie Holen, Susan Martin, Beth Nelson, Gabriel Furtado, Jeff Yeckel, Storm Walker, Perry Haaland, Hugh Robertson, Juan Romano, Bernard Ussher, Robert Daniel, David Volk, Jim Clark, Jeff Talmadge, Alison Moore, David Palmer, Emily Bunning, Joshua Kane, Chad Herzog, Jeff Corle, Kayla Oelhafen, Robert Baird, Tia Regan, Beth Nelson, Scott Sparling, John Freeman Jr., Michael Alexander, John Bunch, Stephanie Smith-Leckness, Hiren Amin. I deeply thank them!

I

Ken Waldman

Keep writing lines
even when there's
no idea beforehand.

Writing isn't exactly
about inspiration.
Let the words
do what they want.
Make poems that
allow surprise. Writers
never trust enough.

On Turning Sixty

Onward, the relentless days, weeks, months —
no chance, hardly, to count haphazard years stacked

tall like firewood cords reaching
up to a barn ceiling. I see now just how
randomly this life has gone,
nothing like I'd imagined. I thought
I'd write novels, teach college, own
nice things, stay put, find a mate,
get married. Instead, some shadowy,

splintery, metaphoric universe
in which my timely pile will one day combust.
X-ray the past to determine what
the flames will consume. For this birthday,
yellow Thai curry, cookies, a bar gig with friends.

Winter Solstice

When the short days feel
inexpressible. When
nothing's left of fall. When
the dark entry of winter makes
each of us shrink. When
relatives finally call.

Some of us burrow. Some
of us bake. Some of us
leave the year behind.
Some of us take. Some of us
travel into the cold,
ice, and snow—the moon's
crescent reminding us to go
easy. We've been here before.

The Northerly
for Kyle Orla

This is how to learn to play fiddle or banjo.
Have a fiddle or banjo, then get it in tune
(early on, find someone to tune it for you).

Next, pick up the instrument every day
on a set schedule, or when you can. Easy does it.
Really, it's like brushing teeth. The thing is
to make it habit. It's one more practice. How
hard is that? Persistence! You just have to play
every day—five or ten minutes, maybe longer.
Really, it's like flossing, shaving, bathing.
Let the music be routine. Patience!
You can't help learning if you give it time.

Tenth Planet Breakdown

for Pat Fitzgerald & Robin Dale Ford

Take a spin on Chena Hot Springs Road.
Evening, and if you know the way,
nothing is like the cool, beautiful universe not on
the usual map, a far studio
happy at the end of a long gravel driveway.

People knock on that door who can
locate the sound of winter
and light, a still and simple world
next to nature, imagination, art.
Enter humbly, or not,
then pull instrument out of case,

be in tune with Mercury, Venus, Mars,
right down to inexplicable Pluto and beyond.
Every album, every track,
a mix of sun, starlight, science
keeping itself amused and at play.
Dig into the cold, the heat. Repeat
once more. A bang. Sometimes lightning
will illuminate the darkness. That's how
new songs and a record come to be.

Arts Midwest

A poem doesn't have to
reach for the heavens
(though it's nice to imagine
something short like this

may change a life—
if only to say go
dance, make music, don't
watch idly, take a walk—for
every moment, yes, can uncover
some extraordinary thing).
The heavens are right here.

Phil and Lisa

Please, a poem about
happiness, finding love
in the place you'd expect—
Lafayette, where people know

any music date can be magic.
Never doubt that sweet woman
dancing, that sweet man playing

lead guitar and bass.
In this marriage we have
something to truly celebrate:
a savory gumbo of passion and grace.

Richard and Anya

Remember all of it, stereo blasting, driving
I-49 to Pineville, I-95 to Boston. Trips to
Cape Breton, Clifftop, Ireland, California.
Happy evenings in Baton Rouge, Eunice, Breaux Bridge,
Arnaudville. Those slow nights staying in
reading or quietly cooking for two. Or maybe
dreaming of a day like this, a Saturday,

a great many of your family and friends gathered,
needing this celebration as the excuse.
Damn, it's finally happening—finally happening

at last. Marriage of fiddle to banjo, guitar to guitar,
necessary music to everything traditional and new.
Yes, remember all of it: everyday together, making
a jambalaya of old-time, Irish, Cajun, and love.

Mississippi Fiddling
for Tim Avalon, Jack Magee, Harry Bolick, et al.

Meridian to Natchez. Olive Branch to Biloxi.
It's a state where the roads make it easy.
Southaven to Oxford. Jackson to Hattiesburg.
Starkville to Tupelo to Clarksdale to Yazoo City.
It's an elderly gentleman tightening the bow,
scratching *Soldier's Joy*. It's a teenaged girl
struggling to master *Grub Springs* or *Wagoner*,
intricate and eccentric double-stops, runs, slides.
Play all morning, all night, all weekend.
Party with a banjo player or guitarist
in the next town or county.

Forget modern pop, piano sonatas, hip hop.
Instead, string-band rags, blues, square dance numbers.
Drunken Hiccups, Rats in the Meal Barrel,
Dusty Miller, Indian War Whoop, Cross-Eyed Gopher,
Little Willie. Some so obscure they're only played
in Charleston. Tonight there's somebody
nearby who's lifting an instrument to play
Goin' up to Hamburg, or *Give the Fiddler a Dram.*

Floyd Country Store
for Dylan Locke

Forget daily concerns, just
let yourself sink into
one of those old songs that take
you somewhere deeply beautiful.
Do you understand? Come listen. You

can hear bluegrass there, plus
old-time fiddle and banjo duets from
up in Rockingham County.
No two fiddlers play the same
tune alike. The music — like
rivers that run through
years, decades, generations.

Sit yourself close if you want. Or maybe
take a place in the back,
order a sandwich, browse
racks of books, CDs, clothes, toys.
Everything's there, especially friends.

Whiskey

for Mark Tamsula, Richard Withers, and Sam Bayard

Where does this music come from?
How to make fiddle and banjo dance
in and out, make sounds sometimes
simple as a single shot of whiskey?
Keep an ear out. You'll soon enough
enter an era tough as these hills. Go back to
Yaugher Holler, near Dunbar, Fayette County.

Pueblo Artists

for Dr. David Volk

People, how can you not be artists here
under a sky so bright, high, and blue,
each day such beautiful foothills
beckoning, a river too. Return to your work,
let yourself go: piano, bass, bassoon,
oboe, viola, voice. This is your place,

a spot to hear a strong world
restless to share its songs.
The music could be anything
if you let it. Listen close.
Sit still. Close your eyes. Imagine
the sound of your breath
shifting into something more.

Jane Turns Fifty

Just wait. How about a new map and plan,
a way to join Idaho, Florida,
North Dakota, Prague, rural Virginia.
Erase sadness, stupidity. You can

tell yourself the truth: it's all about land.
Understand Ohio, West Virginia,
Rhode Island too. New Hampshire, Canada,
New Zealand (why not?), western Maryland.
So many places: rivers, mountains, light.

For god sakes: poems, stories, family, friends.
If you've made it this far, you may well last
fifty more. Your work: to smile, laugh, teach, write,
to be a sunny presence to the end.
Your latest birthday: how the miles race past.

Lenny and Rachel

Love? Certainly love
every day and love every
night. Tender, tender times.
Nature? Certainly hiking,
yes, and biking, skiing,

and sometimes boating.
No, don't forget the best
dogs in the entire world,

Rocky and Rosie, running, jumping,
always welcome, always dear.
Can you imagine the perfect
house? Lenny and Rachel have
envisioned a most wonderful space.
Love? Yes, and now marriage.

Bernard and Rubia

Best never to overthink—
every day is such a rare,
rich blessing when you wake
next to your beloved. How
a decade can run by,
race past like the loveliest
dance. That's it. Don't overthink—

and never let go. No,
never let go because such fast
days, each like a two-step—

right foot, then left foot
(unless it's left foot, then right).
Best not to overthink this.
Instead simply celebrate a decade
as one most perfect slow dance.

Tom's Fiddle and Bow

Take Highway 31 north from Breaux Bridge
or 93 east from Grand Coteau. You can't
miss Arnaudville, that dear old village
set where the Teche meets Bayou

Fuselier. Park your car, wander
into several friendly shops.
Don't skip a plate lunch at Russell's.
Don't miss coffee with new friends at
Little Big Cup. Don't forget
every month's first Sunday afternoon jam

at the fiddle shop down the street. You
never know what local or out-of-towner will
decide to bring fiddle, accordion, guitar,

bass, banjo even. The music is
open to anyone wanting to listen or play.
What do you say? You're invited!

Johnny Appleseed

Just a long-ago American
on a mission. That's how
he became legend. Always
natural, a nurseryman, not some
new and fancy abomination.
Yesterday's rambler, happy

ambling in wood and dirt,
perfectly content barefoot.
Pennsylvania, Ohio, Indiana,
loving the land, practicing
ecstasy through tree and critter.
Some might say the first
environmentalist. He made
each day special simply
doing his own holy work.

This is Some of What I Do

There's a lesson
how in some poems —
in this one too! —
some greater force

is at work,
something unfathomable,

something immense,
or at least something
missing in
every day discourse

or routine.
Find your own way in.

When I started
here, this poem,
all I had were letters
to guide me

into words.

Down I went
on the page, ever hopeful.

II

Change + Change^2

Correct me if I'm wrong
How does one remake
a life? Walk to any
near intersection. Look up.
Give yourself permission to rise,
entering clouds, then space.

+

Choose the farthest arc,
happy for this new path,
another land, be it Iowa,
New Mexico, Michigan,
Georgia. You'll zig, zag —
every step your practice.

Word of South[2]

What do we know
of change? We go
read deeply, hear
deeply, look hard.

One direction is to
follow the heart. Of

such basic ideas
our lives can go
untold ways. You
turn to what's next—
hope's bright path.

Wabash Rotary Club

Who's here, I ask. And I'd guess
a group of men and women who
believe in place, who believe
a group like this matters. No
small thing, sharing ideas that
have an impact. Who's here:

readers, I'd guess. Talkers. Professionals.
Of course, parents and grandparents.
Talented gardeners. Good cooks
and card players. Maybe golfers,
runners, tennis players. Maybe
you, whose greatest joy is helping others

come to see that they, too, can
live here and make a difference.
Useful each week to gather for a meal
before returning to the other work.

Ginger Hill Farm Retreat

for Mayumi Oda

Give visitors a few days here
in tropical island time. Almost
no difference between five minutes or fifty.
Give visitors a few weeks here—
each week like a single long day.
Relaxed hours, even though a single

hour can pass like a minute
in ripe fruity dream. Lilikoi?
Lychee? The plenitude almost
lets you forget papaya, mango, pineapple.

For those visitors open to
a deeper exploration—so many
roots, vines, branches, leaves.
Maybe you remember where you can

reach for an avocado. Or a coconut.
Everywhere a wild, lush land
that's metaphor for what's growing inside you.
Roots, vines, branches, leaves—such thick
earth of tree and bush leading to water and sky.
A place to realize your next life,
too, can be full of truth, beauty, and abundance.

McKean County

Music in the sky, the hills —
clouds make music too.
Keep listening. There's music
everywhere — rivers, lakes,
a forest, a clearing. There's
nothing that's not music.

Can you hear the wild?
Open yourself to everything
underneath. There's
nothing that's not music —
the dirt, the rocks,
your history on earth.

Susquehanna County

Some March days we'll look
up at a gray sky threatening
snow and think: enough winter.
Quickly we slip into April.
Usual here is the unusual.
Everyday weather: easy,
hard, in between. Always
an adventure. Maybe clear cool
nights full of stars. Maybe
nice soft rain. Maybe big wind,
a tree-shaking storm, branches down.

Colors? Green, of course. Yellow,
orange, pink. A muddy brownish
ugly slush in spots. All of it
normal, which is why we love
this place no matter what. Spring arrives
year after year. Our home is alive.

Central Lakes College

Choose a direction, take a step,
eyes and ears open, hoping.
Notice what you've so often missed,
then notice more, so there you are,
reading wind and cloud exactly
as if studying for a test.
Let yourself breathe in the air

like you've never breathed before,
a big slow inhalation, then exhalation,
keeping time like a drum. Is this body
even yours, you wonder. We're all big
slow books, reading one another,

counting the minutes and hours
over and over. We never stop
longing, never stop loving, never stop
learning what we most need to know.
Every day so many lessons, the air
gorgeous with hope. Breath. Step.
Eyes, ears, and now heart opening wider.

Elon University

Everyday, more chores to
leave until tomorrow, or next week,
or maybe next month, this your
never-ending task. Near-impossible to begin

unless you make a list.
Nothing come to mind? Start with one
insignificant, simple act. First, write it.
Very good. That will give you
enough reason to actually commence.
Ready? There's always so much
stuff to get to, so much to finish.
It gets easier the more you cut
through clutter. Success is moving
yourself forward, step by step by step.

CSU Pueblo[2]

Can it be music, mathematics, maybe a magic
so often missing in the everyday use of words?
Understand this is about your life and how you

prepare for what's out there, some strange crap
underneath the surface. So many classes. You
enter each one and never know if this is where
beliefs change, and there it is, like a light bulb
lit bright, making every day shine. Your school
offers an opportunity. The choice: whether to go.

Shelbyville Strand

Sometimes we wonder
how we can continue
each cold, rainy unjust day.
Love is one answer.
Beauty, another. Somehow
years pass as we overcome
various challenges in our
ingenious ways. We fight pain,
loss, ice, flood. Grievance. Yet,
let us celebrate what's most
essential: a place here that

spotlights brilliant music, film,
theater, dance, comedy, a city that
realizes, yes, we've kept alive
an old historic stage where
nothing stops love and beauty. Nothing
denies our communal humanity.

River House

Richer than billionaires
if you define wealth like this:
vivid characters, wickedly fine music
every week, a community
redefining how to really live.

Here's humor, depth, a taste
of elsewhere. You can't make it
up, how friends gather, how
strangers become friends, how
everything fits, how fortunate we are.

Cortez Cultural Center

Clear sky, thin air, a land
opening itself as spirit,
restlessness masquerading
this time as wind.
Each day a revelation—
zillions of possibilities.

Can we ever say what's
up ahead? Certainly
lots of rock, altitude, native
toughness. Desert's sparse
unity. Historic wilderness.
Rich extremes (busy clouds).
A beautiful dump of snow.
Little did we know how

change could lord over
everything. Birds
never sang so well.
Trees never knew such
earth. Drought? A surprise
river of activity. Look! We glisten!

Willowtail Springs

Where do we find
inspiration? Is it getting
lost—literally losing ourselves in woods—
(letting in that old lesson
of staying open to moment,
whatever the circumstance)? Is it
through simple observation?
A distant mountaintop? A bird
in near juniper? How light
lifts everything (how dark descends)?

Simple, isn't it, to simply be,
pursuing what's next. A book to
read (or write). Music to make (as
if in dream). Sketching. Painting.
Notating. A lake. A flower. Rocks.
Green. Gray. Blue. Another bird.
Sky. Water. Land. Dirt.

Route 50 + Route 50²

Ribbon of road across
our state. It climbs
up over passes, connects
Tahoe to Fallon to
Eureka to Ely.

5 states east is Illinois.
Oh, it's a long, lonely ride.

+

Roaring truck or car
on its speedy way to
urgent business. You
take this road and sit
energized. You'll see.

50 becomes 70, 80, 85,
or 90 mph. Sacramento!

Edmonton[2]

Exactly what defines this place?
Depends on who you'd ask. I'd
mention oil, culture, land, a gem
of a Fringe event. Here's how to
navigate this wild festival town.
Take your chances. Go see what
only you can experience here. So
no excuses. Go watch, and listen.

Montana + Dear Butte[2]

More light. Superior sky.
One August I drove west into dusk
near Livingston on 90, the haze
totally surreal. Exceptionally
awful smoke—the shape of our fragile
nature. Today, January. Cold.
A winter sunset to celebrate.

+

Downtown, the crazy old
energy. It was a long time
ago on this hill—Montana
ridiculously rich in copper,

big wide streets a vast web
under tireless sky. Yes, you
take in this history. What it
teaches: you own your past—
every story is deep dark ore.

Zu Gallery

Zinfandel, malbec, cabernet—whether feeling
up or down, let us not forget how

good wine, art, and people keep us civilized
and sane. Listen, friends, it's too easy to
lose ourselves in today's unhappiness.
Life can be cruel and unfair, can brutally kick
exactly where it hurts most. Pain? Suffering?
Rather than wallow, come sip a red, take in this space,
yes, where we can see, and be seen, through artists' eyes.

Turquoise Raven

Thanks for fine art so we better
understand our place here. Thanks for
rain that sustains rivers. Thanks for
quiet so we might finally see
up into and through clouds. Thanks for
open skies that show us
immensities. Thanks for
sandpiper, woodpecker, owl,
eagle, hawk, hummingbird,

rabbit, elk, cougar, bear. Thanks
again for art—poetry and music too—
vital and ineffable force
each of us have within,
next to our heart.

Teller County

There's history here—
everywhere you see it.
Listen too—and sense the ghosts,
little ones, big ones, shy ones.
Every so often you're jolted,
realizing how spirits

can fly you back
over time. You and I—
us—making our own history here
near so much gold,
the element of so many dreams.
Yes: gold, dreams, this mammoth space.

Mountain Home + Mountain Home, Idaho

Most days in this valley —
ordinary extraordinary busyness.
Unless you live here, you won't know.
Nothing to do, you say? Come on,
that's your fault. After school,
a kid can take music lessons, or play
in a sports league. An adult can learn
new skills. There are opportunities

here you won't find in Boise.
Opportunities? That's a treasure.
Mostly it's the Idaho sky telling you:
every busy day is rich with promise.

+

Months of cold. Months
of heat. Always a keen
understanding of weather.
Nothing ever surprises —
there's snow, wind, thunder,
and hail. Lightning too.
It's all in the sky. Yes,
nothing ever surprises.

Here we're prepared for
one forecast, only to
meet another. This week?
Everything is possible.

If you read this, you know
days of cold, days of heat,
and days of surprise. Say
hello to today's weather.
One thing for sure: it's April.

Blaine County

Before the tourism,
long-time locals used to inhabit
a different pace. It was slower then
in so many ways. But always
nature, a grand alpine wild.
Every season, so many visitors

come to enjoy the beauty
of a singular, astonishing valley.
Up they come from California,
New York, Texas. No matter.
The truth is, like wine, it takes
years to best savor this land.

Salina, Kansas

Some days you think you've found
a center here, the middle of everything
loving and true, especially if you look up
into the sky, wondering what
next. Such an honest place,
a land like no other if only you

keep working, keep weeding, keep
an eye on the weather. What
next? Reseeding? A second planting?
Spinach and kale? Keep your heart open,
an ear to the ground. Listen. If you
sense your own self growing, rejoice.

Coffeyville, Kansas

Choosing where to go next, our
ongoing challenge. East or west?
Front or back? Now or later?
Fast or slow? So many questions.
Every intersection, a time to reflect.
Yesterday provides an answer, maybe,
very likely even, that is,
if you know how to truly
learn from past experience.
Let's imagine outcomes —
every intersection a time to reflect.

Keep imagining until you have
an intuition, a hunch, an inkling.
New feelings emerge. Can we
somehow trust them? Do we ever have
a choice? Where do we go next?
Somehow our lives make their own sense.

Montgomery County

Mighty Kansas near-corner county—
Oklahoma, Missouri, Arkansas
nearby. Coffeyville vs. Independence,
that essential and enduring classic
gridiron rivalry. This must be
one of the best places.
Mighty Kansas near-corner county—
each of you here know sky,
river, field, farm, crop, cloud, rain.
You know your land.

Can you tell me now how
old the trees, the lakes, the wind.
Up the road, a place like Iola is
not the same Kansas.
This is your home.
You know your land.

Weatherford, Oklahoma

Wind? But of course!
Expect breezy weeks here,
an occasional gust
that blasts us
halfway to Hydro.
Expect the rare
ridiculous whirlwind
flinging patio chairs,
or a freaky gale
raining hail. My god,
dare we pronounce zephyr

or chinook? The world
keeps breathing down—
long, loud, slow, soft.
An airy world blowing
hot, cold, fast, completing
one day, then the next,
making this our life.
A journey rich with wind.

Marion, Illinois

More murals please,
an abundance like and unlike
river or mountain — this city-wide
inspiration. Behold history
on brick. Art and music, too.
New, old, copper, pink,

indigo, maroon, the colors
like childhood crayon days —
lavender, lilac, lime.
It's the town's big, proud
neighborly face, its bright
outdoor pleasure. Visit
in summer light, winter chill.
Stroll beside, then into wonder.

Fruitdale Farm + WWOOFers

for Fruitdale Farm and its WWOOFers
past, present, future

Finally a moment to pause, perhaps view
rabbit, raccoon, bees pollinating
up close, perhaps a worm
inching in wet dirt. A moment
to think of what's next, one incredible
day after another. Maybe
an afternoon at work in that
lovely new tiny house.
Evening, beer, sauna, friend.

Finally you're caught up, you think,
and a minute later you laugh,
realizing you're mistaken again. But no
mistaking how you love it, all of it.

+

Who are they?
What are their aims
(or should we say dreams)?
One might have come to
find peace in chores. Another,
epiphanies in dirt and compost,
realizing deep hard work
satisfies beyond delight.

Lakewood + Lakewood²

Little did we know how
a pandemic could shape us.
Kids stuck in their homes
every day for weeks asked,
When will this be
over? We all asked—young,
old, those of us in our prime.
Don't despair. We're here today.

+

Let's think how really special
a place this is. Here's an idea—
keep to lakes, woods, a park.
Explore eagles, owls, a whole
world of flight. How to know
ourselves? It's knowing how to
observe nature. So what to do?
Describe what's local and wild.

Elko^2 + Elko^2 + Galveston

Exceptional climate
long on sky. You'll
keep coming back,
or you'll aspire to.

+

Each instance we
let someone fail,
know that a dark
ogre tells us hello.

+

(Gritty beach
and budget motel.
Lose yourself in wine,
vodka, prescription pills.
Every day, the reward —
some mini epiphany.
Tomorrow, always the hope
of change. But no.
Now is never tomorrow.)

Mojave Desert

Millions upon millions
of acres. Pinyon pine, juniper,
Joshua tree. Yucca Valley, China Lake,
Adelanto. Hot. Cold. Dry. Both
vacant and vibrant. A wondrous
empty beauty. Did I say hot, cold,

dry? How about quixotically rich,
exotically varied. Space. Wind.
Sky. Neon. A sublime immensity.
Every mile the possibility of
raw surprising truth. Mesquite,
Tehachapi, Death Valley, Needles.

III

Obituaries

One thing after another. Our years of
bother, joy, desperation, anger, love, sport
in an incomprehensibly random universe.
Then it's over, whether a slow methodical
undertaking, or the sudden fatal boom.
And next come so many words
regarding the life. Stories told, retold
in gatherings of family, friends, colleagues.
Every newspaper marks the passage
since the world keeps score, remembering.

Kerry Blech

King of curiosity, fiddler, seeking
every last thing within tunes. So you
read further, go deeper into those rare
recordings on vinyl, tape, CD.
Years of this. You don't stop

because there are always more almost-
lost gems, so much exceptional,
extraordinary, arcane music to share.
Curious? This is exactly how to
have lived with purpose and satisfaction.

Al Berard

A Cajun man knows how to fix things.
Let me explain. Back some years,

before he passed, I had Al
engineer a CD in his new studio. We
recorded quickly, then mixed.
All good, but for a track with slipshod ending. Al
reset mic, then sat grinning behind drum kit. He came
down hard on cymbal, making the fix with a crash of joy.

Mark Palms + Joe Hall

Master musician
and teacher. Raisin Picker
rhythm. Old-time Michigander
keeper of Cajun and Creole.

Played superbly —
and sang exquisitely.
Loyal to family
most of all. He was,
simply, a gem.

+

Just natural, pure, deep,
only him being him,
essence exactly —

his pulse, his voice,
accordion as truth,
lovely humility,
let us remember.

Ray Garrity

Rest easy, fiddler, guitarist,
accordion player, singer. Oh,
you made so many people

glad. Homer, Fairbanks, Juneau,
Anchorage—all happier when you arrived.
Rest easy, generous and loving partner.
Rest easy, Visa quester extraordinaire.
It's not fair, mortality.
Talkeetna, Cantwell, Pelican, Hope.
You made so many people glad.

Buddy Tabor

Best to listen closely, people.
Underneath the grumbling —
damn physical pain, damn government,
damn stupid music business —
years spent making near perfect

turns of guitar, lyric, voice.
At least a man has that.
Best to listen closely
out of respect. Yes, people,
respect. It's in every true song.

John Caouette

Just when we've heard enough
of the saddest stories, we
hear another. No, we say.
No way. This couldn't be,

couldn't have happened like that.
A kind, generous husband, father, friend
out for a simple, easy jog
under a simple, easy autumn sky,
easy and simple as always. Only
the easy, simple, little mid-run hop and jump
turned into twenty-five-foot fall —
each of those last milliseconds an eternity.

Jeff Day, Pilot

Jamming two full lives in one,
everything a man could want: loving
family, a frontier home with wild music
friends who played tunes fast. Work meant

daily adventure, an excuse to rise
above clouds, view what few could.
You flew past us all, pilot,

passionate to find heaven.
It seemed so beautiful, a third
life so high it felt like wide
open dream. Then you went down,
taking so much with you.

Frank Soos

Finicky with words, he rearranged,
rearranged, rearranged yet again
and again. He sang a Southern
Northern song because his deep
knowledge was Southern and Northern

(somehow living as Down East Westerner too).
Oh, he could be so slowly deliberate
one moment, wickedly quick the next.
So contradictory, especially with endings.

Marni Ludwig

Maybe you're home, that far land where
a smart poem can solve you. That far land
ready and rich as hell, where
no one lacks for sex, where
irony is omnipotent. How you've

looked for that land, lost girl who so
understood the language of misunderstood
demons and dolls. It's that last land past
words. How you'll love it and hate it.
It's home because your tough
genius was never ever enough.

Robin Metz

Reckless and cautious at once —
or, rather, teacher yet student.
Best to accept that
in his sweet and generous way
no telling what might follow.

Maybe one word. Maybe two hundred.
Everything was possible. We'll miss
that full embrace of play. Forever learning,
zealous man, always asking why.

Pat Henry

Perhaps it was all mysterious mist and drizzle,
a thoroughly early October Juneau morning.
Though perhaps a brilliantly clear, cool late afternoon.

How about sudden wind, Texas heat, an impossible autumn
electrical storm—blue lightning to mark the transit.
Nevertheless, he's gone. Gone. Here's what
remains: such matter-of-fact music, so many
years of friendship, goodness, beauty, love.

Betsy Ellen Brown

Beautiful girl, beautiful
exceptional woman and wife.
Terrifically smart, sassy,
simply herself, each sweet
year becoming ever more so.

Every day, blessing upon blessing.
Lover of family, husband, land.
Lover of flower, food, fiddle tune.
Every day, more music.
Not enough time. But time enough.

Beautiful girl, beautiful
remarkable woman, healer
of home, community, office.
Why, we ask. Such beauty,
no, not lost, now within all.

Rosalind Gnatt

Rich in warmth. And rich in heart
of course. The finest model of
serenity, so in keeping with
a true master of divinity. Rich in
love, loyalty, joy. Rich, too, in
intellect: knew opera, banjo, bible, bargain
New York condo listings. Three daring
daughters, five darling grandchildren, one

gallant, gracious husband who
now will so grieve his beloved
and most special spouse. Sadness
transports us, takes us her way.
There she is, forever singing.

F. Wayne Scott

Forgive us, Lord, for

when a loved one passes, we
ask ourselves: *What next?*
Years of devotion lead to this
necessary song that catches
every sad note. It's hard

sometimes. Forgive us, Lord. We
can't undo time. Yet how is it
one day can go on for weeks,
then months? Tears are the oldest
tune. He's now the music of light.

IV

Modern Acrostics

Moon like a hammock
or a thinly crooked smile,
depending on perspective.
Everything depends on perspective —
really, we're all about shade.
No more of these

absolutely terrible times
crossing t's, dotting i's, following
rules of another time and place.
Of this I can be
sure: we're only humans
trying to do what's right even
if we, too, wax and wane. How
can we endure? The moon
sleeps, smiles, suggests.

Modern Acrostics

Maybe Pad Thai,
or perhaps a smart
dinner of
Ethiopian — that
relaxed finger food.
Natural now to imagine

a diet from so many
cultures. Chile
relleno? Lox
or other deli
staples? Pho Ga
topped with basil?
If we're what we eat,
can we stop diversity?
Sushi, salsa, spanakopita.

Modern Acrostics

Meet your shadow?
Open your front
door, peek outside.
Exit cautiously,
realizing this is
not yesterday.

Any door—your
choice. Tomorrow
remains. And today.
One step. The next.
Stand tall, my sister.
This is it, my brother.
If you do this, you
can, indeed, do anything.
So, why do you wait?

Modern Acrostics

More than puzzle
or exercise, the form
defies form. Like trees,
each piece a system of
root, branch, seed, fruit.
Nest, too, maybe, as well

as further possibility.
Climb if you can.
Reach a spot to rest,
or scramble like a squirrel
straight to the top.
This is new and old.
It's an infinity of rings.
Cut? Dry? Stack? Build?
Summon the self, and continue.

Modern Acrostics

Mercy, mercy, mother
of god, another long, cold,
dark winter day, Where's
ecstasy? Where's comedy?
Remember when neither cold
nor dark could stop you?

An insight. Chop wood,
carry water, the cabin years now
replaying within —
one year in Juneau, three in Fairbanks.
Stories, you wrote stories then.
The poems, afterthoughts.
Isn't it all the same, though, in the end?
Counting syllables, words, lines, crafting
sentences, pages, making a whole.

Modern Acrostics

March, June, July —
onward the months.
Damn the months —
each of them
repeating the news,
new and old.

August, September, October —
can we believe the awful
rain, humidity, heat
of these days?
Sometimes we want
to wholly burn
it, this relentless
calendar that marks
so much hard misery.

Modern Acrostics

Mercury, Venus,
our destructible Earth,
doing what Earth does, supporting
earthlings running around,
robbing seas, skies, seeds.
Nothing, it seems, is immune,

although our species also
cannot let our core
resources die. Imagine a satellite
out past Mars, Jupiter,
Saturn, Neptune, Uranus, Pluto,
the unnamed others.
If we can imagine that,
can we imagine our own
serpentine path to safety?

Modern Acrostics

Mornings are a time
of reflection. Afternoons
demand a different mind.
Evenings, too, have their
rhythm. And our dreams —
never forget our dreams.

A dream image for you —
clouds like giant bubbles
rising from a garden.
Or another — seashells
softly falling from
the sky like rain.
Inside each dream,
countless more.
Simply give yourself time.

Modern Acrostics[2]

Mostly, I race from poem to poem.
Or else practice a much slower go,
doing lines word by word by word.
Each of us have a system. We write,
realizing there's no one way. Gather.
Notice. Observe (yes to observation

and plain stick-to-it-ness). A comma,
coming at a right time, can be music.
Red, green, blue, pink. Proper color
or sound (consonant, vowel) can do
such lifting. It can feel so ridiculous,
though, all this effort for what result.
I keep at it because I must, because I
can't not offer my voice, some basic
structure and sense. I have my needs.

Modern Acrostics

Music parties
out in the country.
Driving string-band sounds,
every corner of the house.
Reckless fiddling,
no-nonsense clawhammer banjo,

a guitar and bass
chugging strong, a scene
richer than rye whiskey
out of a silvery flask.
Sail Away Ladies and *Cumberland Gap.*
The Girl I Left Behind Me.
In another corner, ragged
C tunes: *Hell Broke Loose in Georgia,*
Saturday Night Breakdown, Stone's Rag.

Modern Acrostics

Millions and trillions
of molecules everywhere.
Death is always close—
each of us knows this,
ready or not. Now orange—
not that you can eat it,

a slippery philosophical
conceit that somehow
recalls rusting lakes, rivers,
oceans, bodies of water that we
sometimes save, sometimes
trash. Everything is
in flux, my millions and trillions
creating this existence. Yours
somehow vibrating in response.

Modern Acrostics

My great regret: taking
on the years without
daring more often to fail.
Every time I dared to
reach further, and fell,
nothing worse than pain.

A conundrum. Failure
can hurt deep. Sharp aches.
Rude, indiscriminate spasms
on top of dull everyday throbs.
Such pain. Though recall
the seasons following,
improbably high happiness
coming unexpectedly —
spirited, generous, true.

Coda

Ken Waldman + The Nomad

Kenneth, two syllables that feel too formal
every time I'm called it (but better than that
negligent, slapdash two syllable *Kenny*,

which makes me cringe). It's taken decades to
at last own this tough Scottish Ken. *Handsome*?
Let me say, yes, I finally accept. *Born of fire*?
Deep within there's been this long slow burn that's
made me *me*. What does it mean? (What does
any name mean?) For now, Ken means accepting
now, the friendships and love that envelope me.

+

Tempting, isn't it,
how we can construct
everything out of words.

Nice words, naughty words,
overbearing words, obedient words
making their way easily
across the page. Or a continent.
Dangerous words, daunting words.

BIO

Ken Waldman has drawn on 40 years as an Alaska resident to produce poems, stories, and fiddle tunes that combine into a performance uniquely his. 12 CDs mix Appalachian-style string-band music with original poetry. 24 books include 17 full-length poetry collections, a memoir, 3 children's poetry books, a creative writing manual, a novel, and this short story collection. Since 1995 he's toured full-time, performing at leading festivals, concert series, arts centers, and clubs, including the Kennedy Center Millennium Stage, Dodge Poetry Festival, and Woodford Folk Festival (Queensland, Australia). For more about Ken Waldman, www.kenwaldman.com and www.trumpsonnets.com. And for more about Ridgeway Press, www.ridgewaypress.org.

Ken Waldman's Books

Men, Women, and Food
Modern Acrostic for Adventurous Teens
Modern Acrostics for Younger Readers
Now Entering Alaska Time
The Writing Party
Sports Page
Trump Sonnets, Volume 8
Leftovers and Gravy
Trump Sonnets, Volume 7
Trump Sonnets, Volume 6
Trump Sonnets, Volume 5
Trump Sonnets, Volume 4
Trump Sonnets, Volume 3
Trump Sonnets, Volume 2
Trump Sonnets, Volume 1
D is For Dog Team
Are You Famous?
As the World Burns
Conditions and Cures
And Shadow Remained
The Secret Visitor's Guide
To Live on this Earth
Nome Poems